PREACHER FROM THE BLACK LAGOON

Rob Suggs

INTERVARSITY PRESS
DOWNERS GROVE, ILLINOIS 60515

InterVarsity Press is the book-publishing division of InterVarsity Christian Fellowship, a student movement active on campus at hundreds of universities, colleges and schools of nursing in the United States of America, and a member movement of the International Fellowship of Evangelical Students. For information about local and regional activities, write Public Relations Dept., InterVarsity Christian Fellowship, 6400 Schroeder Rd., P.O. Box 7895, Madison, WI 53707-7895.

Cover illustration: Rob Suggs

ISBN 0-8308-1333-0

Printed in the United States of America ∞

Library of Congress Cataloging-in-Publication Data

Suggs, Rob.
    Preacher from the Black Lagoon/Rob Suggs.
       p.   cm.
    ISBN 0-8308-1333-0
    1. Christian life—Humor. I. Title.
  PN6231.C35S84 1992
    741.5'973—dc20   91-33657
                                 CIP

15	14	13	12	11	10	9	8	7	6	5	4	3	2	1
03	02	01	00	99	98	97	96	95	94	93	92	91		

FOR SALLY

a <u>real</u> work of art.

Introduction

Goliath, Paul, Moses and a modern-day pastor tell their side of the story.

Moses: I've called you all together to discuss a festering sore on the face of religion.

Pastor: I'm only a doctor of theology. Perhaps a good dermatologist might be of more assistance?

Paul: Dr. Luke, my traveling companion, comes with my highest recommendations. I had this thorn in the flesh one time, and he . . .

Moses: No, no, no. Back up! I was using a metaphor.

Goliath: What is metaphor? New weapon? Make enemy back up? Goliath must try!

Moses: I was talking about these Christian cartoonists.

Paul: Ah! An abomination! I'd rather put up with the Roman army.

Moses: Exactly. All of us in this room are under attack by these people.

Goliath: Attack? Then Goliath suggests we gird up loins, grab metaphors and go do battle! Kill wives and children also!

Paul: Thank you, my friend, but no. If we have not love, we are nothing.

Pastor: I think the big guy might be onto something. What's your plan, Goliath?

Moses: Please! You can't just wipe them out. These people keep coming at you like the Philistines.

Goliath: Like who?

Moses: Um, the *Phillies team!* Yes, the Philadelphia Phillies.

Pastor: The *Phillies* keep coming at you?

Moses: Never mind. The important thing is, we used to get respect. I was once sculpted, for example, by Michelangelo. There was an artist!

Paul: I think you're missing the point. The wisdom of this age, as I remarked in my masterful First Epistle to the Corinthians, is foolishness in God's sight. Is it not fitting, then, that we appear as fools for Christ?

Pastor: Well, the cartoonist did a good job of making *you* a fool for Christ in this one! Look at the nose!

Har, har . . .

Paul: What's this? I'll kill the ungodly heretic!

Goliath: And Goliath go with you!

Moses: Settle down, fellas. I won't have you breaking my sixth commandment.

Pastor: Besides, this cartoonist is *six foot two.* You ancients were smaller people since there were no Nautilus machines.

Paul: I can do all things through Christ which strengtheneth me!

Moses: Hey, he's taking himself out of context! That's kind of interesting.

Pastor: What bothers *me* is that it's a further devaluation of the ministerial image. Television, movies and novels have all conspired to undermine our clerical respectability. Pastors today are viewed in popular culture as ninnies. At worst we're money-grubbing monsters, and at best we're well-meaning incompetents! Just look at these cartoons. One would be led to believe (point number one). We prattle on ad nauseum (point number two). And that our sermons put people to . . . put people to . . . *guys?*

Others: Zzzzzzzzzzzzz . . .

The Author arrives.

Author: What have we here, pastor? Normally one uses Bible characters to put *others* to sleep, yet it appears you've succeeded in sedating *the material itself!* Remarkable. I must draw it sometime.

Pastor: They're not sleeping! They're taking a page from *you* and trying to get my goat!

Goliath: Who got goat? Goliath hungry for snack!

Paul: Looking over my epistles (which impress me anew at each reading), I find that *cartooning* is nowhere found among any of my lists of spiritual gifts. So who says you're God's gift to religion, young man?

Author: Certainly not me.

Paul: Why, therefore, do you persist in drafting these vile etchings?

Author: Because I believe in (1) utilization of satirical tradition to enhance theological insight; (2) utilization of clinically proven medication known as *laughter;* and (3) I can utilize the bucks.

Goliath: Goliath no understand foreign tongue of 6′2″ man.

Paul: It's not Greek to me, either.

Moses: Well, here's a fancy word we all understand—sacrilege! In my day we would have turned you into a pillar of salt or maybe ink!

Author: You're taking this thing too personally. Let's think about this whole humor thing. Take the Ten Commandments. . . .

Moses: I already did. Everybody ignored me.

Author: But I don't! Number three says don't misuse the Lord's name. And I don't! Number two says nix on idol worship, so I take aim at every sacred cow I can. Hey, it's trivia time. Do you know where we get that phrase "sacred cows"?

Moses: Don't push it.
  What's your point?

Author: The Lord is to be reverenced—Father, Son and Holy Spirit. But anyone from the apostles on down is fair game.

Paul: Which includes you, too, my friend.

Author: Well, um, I . . .

Moses: Hey, look, he's blushing! I wonder, what would make a Baptist humorist blush?

Pastor: "Baptist humorist" is an oxymoron.

Paul: Just a simple "moron" will do.

Author: Leave my denominational affiliation out of this.

Pastor: *Aha!* Cartoonists who live in glass houses shouldn't throw stones.

Goliath: *Stones???* Who said stones?

Pastor: Now, just calm down, big fellow. Your head made a hole in the ceiling! I didn't mean to mention "stones" in your presence. It was the last thing that entered my mind. . . .

(Sudden end of interview.)

CARTOON TESTIMONIES

A Visit from the Late Night Sermon Pixies

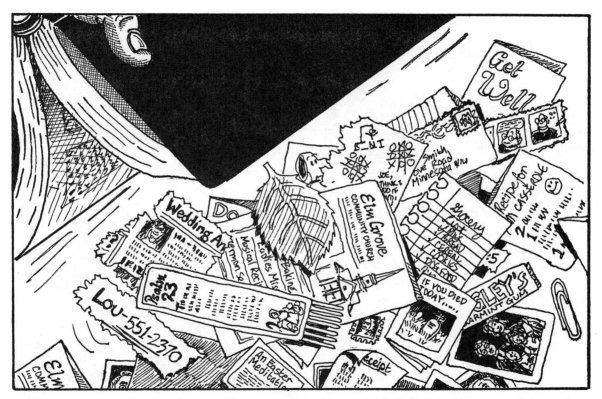

BIBLIDUE: (Bĭb'·lĭ·dōō) *n.* THAT DIVERSE CONGLOMERATION OF UNEXPLAINABLE ITEMS WHICH COLLECTS IN EVERY BIBLE.

FEW SUSPECTED THAT THE PASTOR OFTEN STAYED AFTER EVERYONE HAD GONE HOME, PUT ON THE BIG BLACK ROBE, AND PLAYED "CAPED AVENGER."

MISS LULU ARRIVES IN HEAVEN

PREACHER'S KID

AS NEW TEACHER FOR THE LADIES' BIBLE CLASS, GLADYS KNEW SHE HAD A HARD ACT TO FOLLOW.

EVELYN SCREAMED; AGNES SWOONED. IT HAD BEEN ASSUMED BY EVERYONE THAT ERNESTO WOULD *NEVER* DARKEN THE DOOR OF THE CHURCH.

ANOTHER SERVICE AT "THE LITTLE CHURCH IN THE WILDWOOD"

YUPPIES OF THE OLD TESTAMENT

IT WAS ONLY THE REV. TOOEY'S FIRST CHURCH, BUT ALREADY HE KNEW HE HAD THE COOLEST PULPIT IN TOWN.

Acme REAR VIEW PULPIT MIRROR

EVERY PASTOR'S SECRET DREAM

DANIEL: THE NIGHTMARE CONTINUES

IN ORDER TO MAKE THE FIRST MISSIONARY OFFERING, EARLY CHRISTIANS
ROB FROM PETER TO PAY PAUL.

FOR 57 YEARS IT HAD BEEN MRS. GRUMPLING'S SEAT IN CHURCH, AND THERE THEY FOUND HER... ANOTHER VICTIM OF PEWTRIFICATION.

YOUNG PAUL WRITES AN EPISTLE FROM CAMP

BOOKS THAT DIDN'T MAKE IT INTO THE BIBLE

JOHN THE BAPTIST MEETS MARVIN THE EPISCOPALIAN

MILTON USES THE PERSONAL TOUCH TO BRING WITNESSING TO LIFE.

ILL-ADVISED ETHNIC JOKES OF THE ANCIENT WORLD

STILL MORE NEW STUDY BIBLES

AT THE TELEVANGELIST REST HOME

MOSES' EARLY WEATHERCASTING CAREER

THAT SUMMER, ROLAND AND ELMER RACKED UP A RECORD 2,317 BEACH CONVERSIONS.

ILL-FATED TRAVEL AGENCIES OF THE OLD TESTAMENT

AT THE MEGACHURCH

TRUCKER CHURCH

SPIRITUAL PICK·UP LINES

ADVANCE PREPARATION, ANOTHER IMPORTANT ELEMENT OF THE SERMON

SCENE FROM THE HIT PHARISEE GAME SHOW, "IS IT LAWFUL?"

THOUGH RELUCTANT TO BE A "PULPIT POUNDER," PASTOR PERKINS HAS HIS OWN METHODS OF COMMANDING ATTENTION.

JOE TURPIN AND HIS PERSONAL DEMONS, TOP ROW (L-R): PASTA, SPEEDING, SHOWING HOME MOVIES TO FRIENDS, LATE MOVIES, WAITING UNTIL APRIL 14 TO FILL OUT INCOME TAX FORMS, NAIL-BITING, COFFEE. **FRONT ROW......**

SUDDENLY MRS. APPLEBY DISCOVERED A KNOB-THINGY SHE HAD NEVER NOTICED, AND IN A TWINKLING WAS BORN THE SOUND THAT CREATED A NEW DENOMINATION.

HYMNASTICS: (Hĭm·nă'·stĭks) n. THAT ATHLETIC EVENT ASSOCIATED WITH HIGHLY EXCITABLE CHORUS LEADERS

CHRISTIANIZING THE CLASSICS

NEW TRENDS IN THE OFFERTORY

WHERE WE GET OUR BIBLES

THE LADIES' BIBLE CLASS AIRLIFTS "PROJECT POTLUCK" TO THE THIRD WORLD.

JOSEPH, HIS FAMOUS COAT, AND SOME OF HIS SHEEP

BEFORE HIS MORE SUCCESSFUL CAREER IN PROSE, THE APOSTLE JOHN TRIES HIS HAND AT SONG-WRITING.

OUTREACH VISITATION BY FAX

AT THE THEOLOGY LAB

GOLIATH HAD A MOTHER, TOO.

SOME OF THE GUYS FROM WORK HELPED DAVID TRAIN FOR THE BIG GOLIATH BOUT.

Updating our Worship Language

THE CHURCHAHOLIC: KNOW THE WARNING SIGNS

THE AUTHOR'S FIRST QUESTION IN HEAVEN